VENUS FLYTRAPS EAT BUGS!

By Barbara M. Linde

Gareth Stevens
PUBLISHING

Please visit our website, www.garethstevens.com. For a free color catalog of all our high-quality books, call toll free 1-800-542-2595 or fax 1-877-542-2596.

Acknowledgements
Many thanks to the following people for their expertise and input:
Richard Curzon, Horticulturist, and Phil Sheridan, Ph.D., President and Director, Meadowview Biological Research Station, Woodford, Virginia; Susie Yager, Virginia Master Naturalist; Meegan Wallace, Botanist, Virginia Master Naturalist

Cataloging-in-Publication Data

Names: Linde, Barbara M.
Title: Venus flytraps eat bugs! / Barbara M. Linde.
Description: New York : Gareth Stevens Publishing, 2017. | Series: World's weirdest plants | Includes index.
Identifiers: ISBN 9781482456400 (pbk.) | ISBN 9781482456431 (library bound) | ISBN 9781482456424 (6 pack)
Subjects: LCSH: Venus's flytrap–Juvenile literature. | Carnivorous plants–Juvenile literature.
Classification: LCC QK495.D76 L56 2017 | DDC 583'.75–dc23

First Edition

Published in 2017 by
Gareth Stevens Publishing
111 East 14th Street, Suite 349
New York, NY 10003

Designer: Katelyn E. Reynolds
Editor: Kristen Nelson and Joan Stoltman

Photo credits: Cover, p. 1 Martin Shields/Science Source/Getty Images; cover, pp. 1–24 (background) Conny Sjostrom/Shutterstock.com; cover, pp. 1–24 (sign elements) A Sk/Shutterstock.com; p. 5 Stefano Zucchinali/ Wikipedia.org; p. 7 (illustration) © iStockphoto.com/nicoolay; p. 7 (photo) Paul Zahl/National Geographic/ Getty Images; p. 9 Adam Gault/OJO Images/Getty Images; p. 11 GUILLERMO LEGARIA/AFP/Getty Images; p. 13 Ed Reschke/Photolibrary/Getty Images; p. 15 Hans Neleman/Photodisc/Getty Images; p. 17 Luigi Masella/EyeEm/Getty Images; p. 19 Humanmap/Wikipedia.org; p. 21 Mint Images - Paul Edmondson/Mint Images RE/Getty Images.

Printed in China

CPSIA compliance information: Batch #CW17GS : For further information contact Gareth Stevens, New York, New York at 1-800-542-2595.

CONTENTS

Words in the glossary appear in **bold** type
the first time they are used in the text.

SNACK ATTACK!

Bright, warm sunbeams shine down on the Venus flytrap. The plant needs food. With roots firmly in the ground, the plant can't hunt or move at all. Luckily, the Venus flytrap has another way to get food!

The plant has leaves that look like a pair of open hands. A curious bug climbs in, stepping between the two parts of the leaf to taste the sweet nectar in the center. SNAP! The leaves are actually a trap that quickly close with the bug caught inside.

This hover fly will make a tasty snack for the Venus flytrap!

5

CLEVER CARNIVORE

Most plants get all their **nutrients** from sun, water, and good things in the soil. But the Venus flytrap lives in poor soil, so it eats meat in the form of bugs for extra nutrition!

The Venus flytrap grows like most other plants, starting as a seed and growing roots into the ground. The flower is about 1 inch (2.5 cm) across and grows high above the traps. This way, **pollinating** bugs, which help the plant spread, won't get trapped and eaten.

SEEDS OF KNOWLEDGE
Meat-eating plants, also called carnivorous plants, eat over 150 types of **insects**!

THE PARTS OF A VENUS FLYTRAP

flower

stem

trap

roots

The traps of a Venus flytrap are only 1 inch (2.5 cm) long, though one **cultivar** of Venus flytrap can grow 2-inch (5 cm) traps!

CAUGHT YA!

The Venus flytrap's traps are actually the leaves. They grow in pretty red, pink, or purple colors to attract, or draw in, insects. The traps also have a coating of sweet nectar that bugs like.

Little spiky hairs called **trigger** hairs stick up from the traps' surface. When a bug touches two hairs within a few seconds or one hair twice in a row, the trap snaps shut. The long, toothlike hairs along the trap's edge, called cilia, begin folding over each other to keep the **prey** inside.

SEEDS OF KNOWLEDGE

The snap of the trap takes about one-tenth of a second—that's faster than you can blink your eyes!

As the trap is closing, the cilia fold over each other so this fly can't escape. Bye-bye, fly!

cilia

trigger hair

9

DIGESTING DINNER

Squirming from panic, the bug hits the trigger hairs a third time, which tells the trap to close tighter. The cilia unfold and stretch out, and the edges of the trap press tightly together. Nothing, not even a drop of rainwater, can get in … or out!

Hitting the trigger hairs five times makes **enzymes** fill the trap. These liquids digest, or break down, the soft, inside parts of the bug. The plant absorbs, or takes in, the nutrients from the bug's body.

The cilia stretch out and the edges tighten, forming a bubble around the bug that will soon be filled with deadly liquid.

SMARTY PLANTS

The more often a bug hits the trigger hairs, the more enzymes a Venus flytrap makes. In other words, if a bug struggles a lot, the plant knows it has to work harder to kill it. The trap also senses how much bug is left to digest and if it needs to make more enzymes.

If nonfood items, like dust or a raindrop, hit a trigger hair, the Venus flytrap can sense it isn't food. How Venus flytraps do this is still a mystery to scientists.

Will this bug be difficult for
the Venus flytrap to eat?

13

ALL DONE!

Digestion takes 5 to 12 days, but bigger bugs take longer and can slow down digestion. Once digestion is done, the enzymes go back into the plant. The same enzymes are used over and over. They get weaker as the trap gets older.

After the enzymes go back into the trap, it opens. The dried-up, unused parts of the bug fall to the ground and get blown away by wind or washed away by rain. The trap is ready to attract new prey again!

There's no way for this bug to escape now!

15

WHAT'S ON THE MENU?

Don't let the plant's name fool you—the Venus flytrap eats a lot more than flies. Spiders, beetles, ants, moths, and baby crickets are all on the menu! As the plant grows, the growing trap can snap up larger and larger prey. Yum!

Each trap is only able to close around seven times. After that, it stays open. After 3 months, the trap and leaf turn black and die. Not to worry, a Venus flytrap grows new traps throughout its life. It's always ready to feed!

SEEDS OF KNOWLEDGE

A daddy longlegs or a grasshopper won't fit all the way into even a full-grown trap. The parts that don't fit rot, which in turn rots the trap. A rotted trap soon turns black and falls off.

This bug is too large for the trap.

17

HOME SWEET HOME

There's only one **species** of Venus flytrap in the world, and its native **habitat** is in and around Wilmington, North Carolina. This area has sandy soil, sun, hot weather, and lots of rain for its 35,000 Venus flytraps! That sounds like a lot, but it's not, considering they don't grow anywhere else in the world!

Venus flytraps need winter **frosts**, too. During winter, the flowers and leaves die, while the roots live underground. The plant regrows in the spring.

SEEDS OF KNOWLEDGE

It's against the law to take a Venus flytrap out of the ground in North Carolina. The fine for stealing is $75 to $150 per plant!

Native Venus flytraps and other carnivorous plants grow in and around Wilmington, North Carolina.

Find Venus flytraps here!

BURN, BABY, BURN

Over the years, the Venus flytrap has become **endangered**. Roads and buildings have destroyed a lot of the Venus flytrap's natural habitat. Thankfully, laws now exist to protect the habitat.

Another problem Venus flytraps can have is trees. When trees get too tall, they block the sun from the Venus flytrap and other low plants. But nature has a solution! Lightning strikes start fires that burn the tall trees, allowing the low plants to get sun again!

SEEDS OF KNOWLEDGE

For years, people put out lightning fires because they were scared and didn't understand. Now, firefighters set the trees on fire on purpose. This is called a controlled burn or prescribed fire, which they watch carefully.

This wetland needed a controlled burn to thrive again.

GLOSSARY

cultivar: a group within a species grown by people to have special features

endangered: in danger of dying out

enzyme: matter made in the body that helps with digestion and other body processes

frost: a covering of tiny ice crystals formed on outdoor surfaces when it gets very cold

habitat: the natural place where an animal or plant lives

insect: a small, often winged, animal with six legs and three body parts

nutrient: something a living thing needs to grow and stay alive

pollinate: to take pollen from one flower, plant, or tree to another

prey: an animal that is hunted by other animals for food

species: a group of plants or animals that are all the same kind

trigger: something that starts a process when it's touched

FOR MORE INFORMATION

Books

Aaseng, Nathan. *Weird Meat-Eating Plants*. Berkeley Heights, NJ: Enslow Publishers, 2011.

Lawrence, Ellen. *Meat-Eating Plants: Toothless Wonders*. New York, NY: Bearport Publishing, 2013.

Rice, Barry. *Monster Plants: Meat Eaters, Real Stinkers, and Other Leafy Oddities*. New York, NY: Scholastic, 2010.

Websites

Carnivorous Plants of Cartwheel Bay
pbslearningmedia.org/resource/etv08.sci.life.evo.carnplt/carnivorous-plants-of-cartwheel-bay/
Watch a video of a naturalist in Cartwheel Bay, South Carolina, home to many carnivorous plants!

Carnivorous Plants—Plants That Eat Meat
easyscienceforkids.com/carnivorous-plants/
Fill up on fun facts about meat-eating plants. Take a quiz to see what you learned.

Venus Flytraps: Jaws of Death
naturesvenusflytrap.weebly.com/venus-fly-trap.html
Watch a slow-motion video of a Venus flytrap catching and eating a fly.

INDEX